Progressive Beginner

KEYBOARD

by
Gary Turner & Peter Gelling

Visit our Website
www.learntoplaymusic.com

The Progressive Series of Music Instruction Books, CDs and DVDs

Published by
KOALA MUSIC PUBLICATIONS ™

Like us on Facebook
www.facebook.com/LearnToPlayMusic

View our YouTube Channel
www.youtube.com/learntoplaymusiccom

Follow us on Twitter
twitter.com/LTPMusic

Visit our Website
www.learntoplaymusic.com

PROGRESSIVE BEGINNER KEYBOARD
I.S.B.N. 978-982-9118-13-4
Order Code: 11813

For more information on the
Learn to Play series contact:
L.T.P. Publishing Pty Ltd
email: info@learntoplaymusic.com
or visit our website:
www.learntoplaymusic.com

Contents

Introduction

Progressive Beginner Keyboard assumes you have no prior knowledge of music or playing the Keyboard. This book will show you:

1. How to play over 25 songs using a range of two octaves.
2. Major, Minor and Seventh chords.
3. 12 Bar Blues and Turnaround progressions.

This book also features a chord chart section with over 50 different chords. After completing the book you will have a solid understanding of the fundamentals of Keyboard playing and be ready for further study on specific styles of playing, e.g., Rock, Blues, etc. **All Keyboard players should know all of the information contained in this book.** The best and fastest way to learn is to use this book in conjunction with:

1. Buying sheet music and song books of your favorite recording artists and learning to play their songs.
2. Practicing and playing with other musicians. You will be surprised how good a basic Keyboard/Drums/Bass/Guitar combination can sound even when playing easy music.
3. Learning by listening to your favorite songs.

Approach to Practice

It is important to have a correct approach to practice. You will benefit more from several short practices (e.g., 15-30 minutes per day) than one or two long sessions per week. This is especially so in the early stages, because of the basic nature of the material being studied. In a practice session you should divide your time evenly between the study of new material and the revision of past work. It is a common mistake for semi-advanced students to practice only the pieces they can already play well. Although this is more enjoyable, it is not a very satisfactory method of practice. You should also try to correct mistakes and experiment with new ideas. It is the author's belief that the guidance of an experienced teacher will be an invaluable aid in your progress.

Know Your Keyboards...

Electric Organ

The electric organ, invented in the 1930s, gained mainstream popularity through models like the Hammond B-3 (pictured), which is used extensively in jazz, blues and rock music. The unique sound is created by 'tonewheels' rotating in front of electromagnetic pickups, and the sound that this produces can be modified through several switches and drawbar combinations to create millions of different tonal variations. Many modern electric organs are digital, although they still share common design traits with original electro-mechanical organs.

Using the Accompanying DVD and CD

The accompanying DVD and CD contain video and audio recordings of each example in this book. An exercise number (as pictured below) indicates a recorded example.

  **57** ⟵ DVD TRACK NUMBER

The book shows you where to put your fingers and what techniques to use, while the recordings let you hear and see how each example should sound and look when performed correctly. Practice the examples on your own, playing slowly at first. Then try playing to a metronome set to a slow tempo until you can play the example evenly and without stopping. Gradually increase the tempo as you become more confident and then you can try playing along with the recording. You will hear a drum beat at the beginning of each example to lead you in and help you keep time.

Included with this book:

• **1 Audio CD**, which can be played in any CD player. It contains every exercise from start to finish so you can hear how each example should sound.

• **1 Video DVD**, which can be played in any DVD player. It begins with an easy-to-use menu where you can find videos of all exercises in the book. Each video shows you how to play the exercise and includes an animated score so you can read and play along. You can also choose between three audio options:

1. **Full track** - hear how the Keyboard should sound with a band
2. **Solo part** - listen to the Keyboard part by itself
3. **Backing track** - play along with the band!

The 'audio streams' (or language tracks) are accessed from the DVD remote.

Tips

* Most DVD and portable media players have the ability to repeat tracks. You can make good use of this feature to practice the examples a number of times without stopping.

How to Sit at the Keyboard

Sit up straight and relaxed. If your seat can move up or down, adjust it to a comfortable height. The instrument shown in **Photo 1** is an Electronic Keyboard, but the sitting position is the same for all types of Keyboard.

Photo 1

Hand Shape

Always curve your fingers. This helps keep your fingers at the same level, as shown in **Photo 2**.

Photo 2

When you play the keys on the Keyboard, use the tips of your fingers, and the side of your thumb. See **Photo 3**.

Photo 3

Music Notes

There are only **seven** letters used for notes in music. They are:

A B C D E F G

These notes are known as the **musical alphabet**. They are the names of the **white** keys on the Keyboard.

The Keyboard

The black keys always appear in groups of two or three. The **C note** is a **white key**. It is always on the left hand side of a group of two black keys. Find all the **C** notes on your Keyboard.

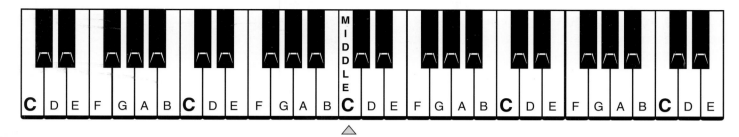

The first note you will learn to play is Middle C.

How to Find Middle C

Middle C is the note in the middle of the Keyboard. Play middle C with the thumb of your right hand.

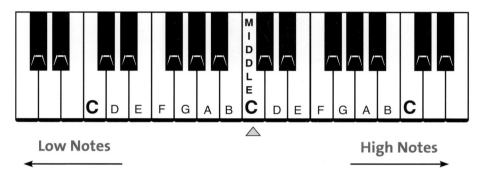

Low Notes

High Notes

Fingers

Each finger has its own number.

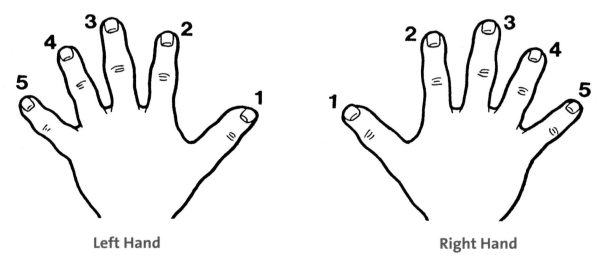

Left Hand

Right Hand

The **thumb** of each hand is counted as the **first** finger and has the number **1**.

How to Read Music

These five lines are called the **staff** or **stave**.
Music notes are written in the spaces and on the lines of the staff.

Treble Clef

This symbol is called
a **treble clef**.

Bass Clef

This symbol is called
a **bass clef**.

Treble Staff

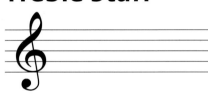

A staff with a treble clef written on it is
called a **treble staff**.

Bass Staff

A staff with a bass clef written on it is called a
bass staff.

High notes are written on the **treble staff**, and are usually played with your **right hand**.
Low notes are written on the **bass staff**, and are usually played with your **left hand**.

The Grand Staff

High Notes
(right hand side of Keyboard)

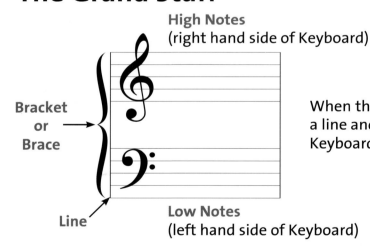

**Bracket
or
Brace** →

Line

Low Notes
(left hand side of Keyboard)

When the treble and bass staves are joined together by
a line and a bracket, they are called a **grand staff**.
Keyboard music is written on the grand staff.

Music is divided into **bars** (sometimes called **measures**) by **barlines**. In this example there are **two** bars of music.

Barline →   **Barline** →

| 1 Bar | 1 Bar |

Note and Rest Values

The following table sets out the most common notes used in music and their respective time values (i.e., length of time held). For each note there is an equivalent rest, which indicates a period of silence.

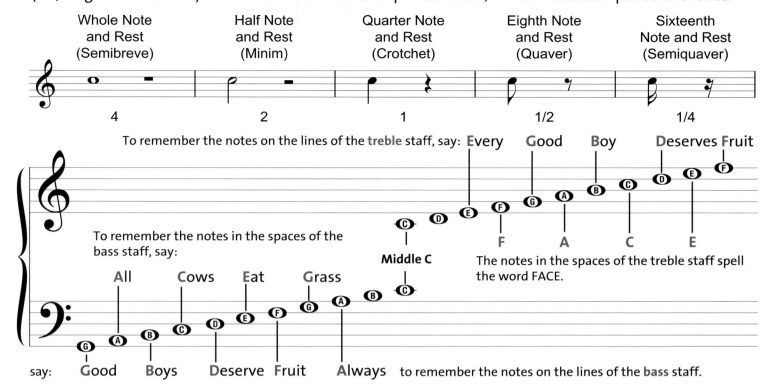

Whole Note and Rest (Semibreve)	Half Note and Rest (Minim)	Quarter Note and Rest (Crotchet)	Eighth Note and Rest (Quaver)	Sixteenth Note and Rest (Semiquaver)
4	2	1	1/2	1/4

To remember the notes on the lines of the **treble** staff, say: Every Good Boy Deserves Fruit

The notes in the spaces of the treble staff spell the word FACE.

To remember the notes in the spaces of the **bass** staff, say: All Cows Eat Grass

say: Good Boys Deserve Fruit Always to remember the notes on the lines of the **bass** staff.

The Quarter Note

stem

note head

This is a musical note called a **quarter** note. A quarter note lasts for **one** beat.

The Four Four Time Signature

The two pairs of numbers after the clefs are called the **time signature**.

This is called the **four four** time signature.
It tells you there are **four** beats in each bar.
There are **four** quarter notes in a bar of ¾ time.

LESSON ONE

The Notes Middle C, D and E

Middle C is written just **below** the treble staff on a short line called a **ledger** line. See page 9 to locate middle C on the Keyboard.

• Middle **C** is played with the **first** finger (thumb) of your right hand.
• The **D** note is played with the **second** finger of your right hand.
• The **E** note is played with the **third** finger of your right hand.

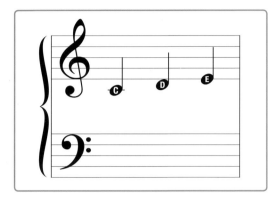

The Quarter Note

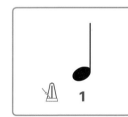

This is a **quarter note**. It lasts for **one** beat. There are four quarter notes in one bar of $\frac{4}{4}$ time.

 **1**

In the following example there are **four** bars of music, **two** bars of **middle C** (bars 1 and 4), **one** bar of the **D** note (bar 2) and **one** bar of the **E** note (bar 3). There are four quarter notes in each bar.

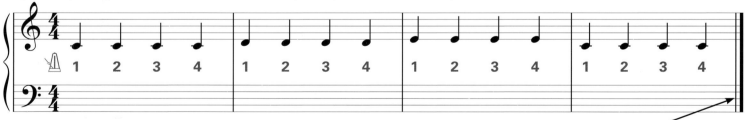

The **double bar** at the end indicates that the exercise has finished.

The Half Note

This is a **half** note. It lasts for **two** beats. There are **two** half notes in one bar of $\frac{4}{4}$ time.

The Whole Note

This is a **whole** note. It lasts for **four** beats. There is **one** whole note in one bar of $\frac{4}{4}$ time.

The **larger** bold numbers in the count indicate that a note is to be played. The **smaller** numbers indicate that a note is to be held until the next bold number (note).

This song contains quarter, half and whole notes. Make sure you use the correct fingers and follow the count carefully.

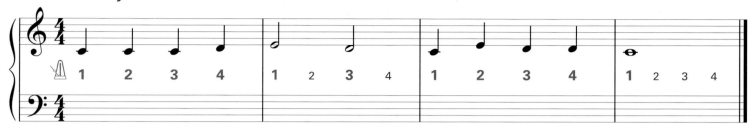

The Notes F and G

• Play the note **F** with the **fourth** finger of your right hand.
• Play the note **G** with the **fifth** finger of your right hand.

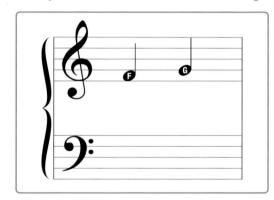

3   Aura Lee

The song **Aura Lee** contains 8 bars of music in ₄₄ time. Remember to count as you play, to help you keep time.

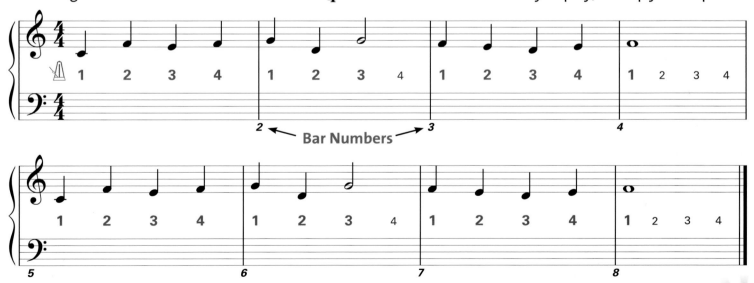

THINGS TO REMEMBER

• Play the keys with the tips of your fingers.
• Keep your fingers curved.

LESSON TWO

Chords

A **chord** is a group of notes which are played together. Chords are used to accompany the melody of a song. Chords are usually played with the **left** hand and the melody is played with the right. The first chord you will learn is **C major**, usually just called the **C** chord.

The C Major Chord

The **C** chord contains the notes **C**, **E** and **G**. To play the **C** chord use the **first**, **third** and **fifth** fingers of your left hand, as shown in the **C** chord diagram.

C	Chord Symbol

C Major Chord

C

Seventh Chords

Another common type of chord is the **dominant seventh** chord, usually called a **seventh** chord. A seventh chord is indicated by the number **7** written after the chord name, e.g.: **G seventh** is written as **G7**. Below is the **G7** chord which contains a new note - the **B** next to the **C** below Middle C.

G7	Chord Symbol

G Seventh Chord

G7

The **G7** chord contains the notes **G**, **B** and **F**. Play the B with the **fifth** finger of your left hand, and use your **first** and **second** fingers to play the G and F notes, as shown in the chord diagram.

Changing Chords

Practice changing between the **C** and **G7** chords. As both these chords contain the same **G** note, changing between them is quite easy because the **thumb** stays in the same position. It is important to always use the correct fingering when playing notes and chords.

www.learntoplaymusic.com

The Whole Rest

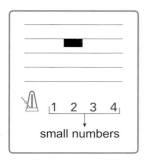

This is a **whole rest**. It indicates **one bar** of silence. A whole rest in 4/4 time is four beats of silence.

Chord symbols are placed above the staff. There are two chords in bar 3. Each of these chords receive **two** beats.

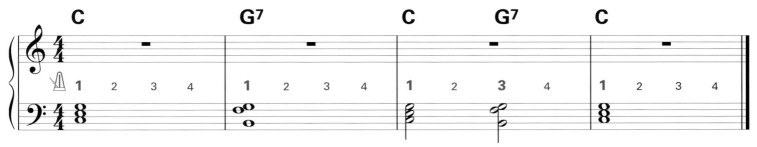

Songs with Chords

Before playing songs with chords, practice each part separately. First practice the **melody** of the song by itself (right hand part), then practice the **chords** by themselves (left hand part). Once you have learned both parts, play them together. Practice slowly and evenly, and count as you play. The part containing the chords is called the **accompaniment**.

▶ 5   Ode to Joy

This song is the main theme to **Beethoven's 9th Symphony**. It contains all the notes and chords you have learned so far and has two chords in bar 8.

Ludwig van Beethoven

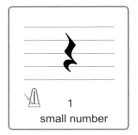

LESSON THREE

The Quarter Rest

This symbol is a quarter rest. It indicates **one beat of silence**. Do not play any note. Remember that small counting numbers are placed under rests.

1
small number

▶ 6 **Good Evening Friends**

One beat of silence

These two dots are a **repeat sign** and indicate that the song is to be played again.

The F Chord

The next chord you will learn to play is the **F** chord. To play the **F** chord, use the **first**, **second** and **fifth** fingers of your left hand, as shown in the F chord diagram. The **F** chord introduces the note **A** below middle C.

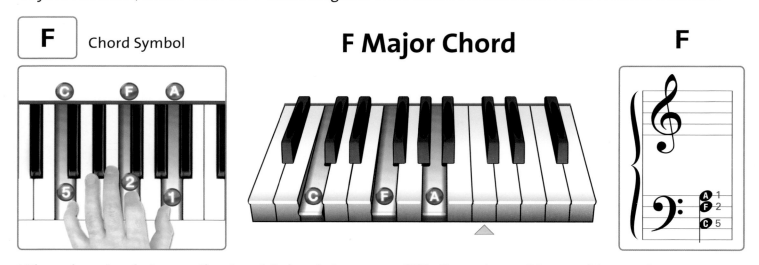

F Chord Symbol

F Major Chord

F

When changing between the **C** and **F** chords keep your **fifth** finger in position as this note is common to both chords. When changing between the **F** and **G7** chords keep your **second** finger in position as this note is common to both chords. Practice changing between **C**, **F** and **G7**.

The Half Rest

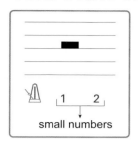

small numbers

This symbol is a **half** rest.
It indicates **2 beats** of silence.

The Lead-in

Sometimes a song does not begin on the first beat of a bar. Any notes which come before the first full bar are called **lead-in notes** (or **pick-up notes**). When lead-in notes are used, the last bar is also incomplete. The notes in the lead-in and the last bar add up to one full bar.

▶ 7   When the Saints Go Marchin' In

When the Saints Go Marchin' In is an early Jazz standard made popular by brass bands in New Orleans. The song uses a lead-in and also contains both quarter and half rests. The **counting numbers** refer to the **melody** (right hand part).

Instead of writing a chord symbol above each bar of music it is common to only to write a chord symbol when the chord changes, e.g., the first 6 bars of this song are a **C** chord.

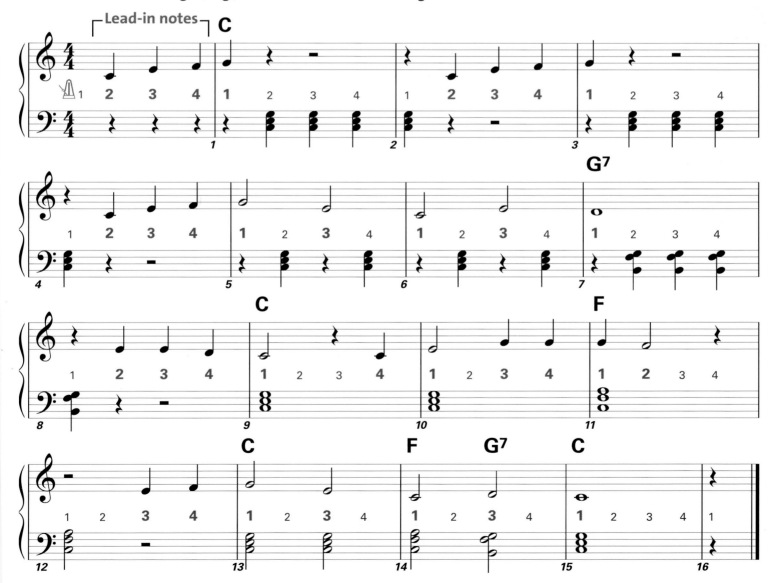

LESSON FOUR

The Three Four Time Signature

This is the **three four** time signature. It tells you there are **three** beats in each bar. There are **three** quarter notes in a bar of ¾ time. Three four time is also known as waltz time.

Time signatures always come after the clef. The **top number** indicates the **number of beats** per bar and the **bottom number** indicates the **length of each beat**.

The Dotted Half Note

This is a **dotted half** note. It lasts for **three** beats. One dotted half note makes one bar of music in ¾ time.

A dot written after a note extends its value by half.

▶ **8   Austrian Waltz**

This song has **dotted half notes** in the left hand part. Once again, the counting numbers refer to the melody (right hand part). From this point on, **all** counting numbers will refer to the melody. The left hand part is the **accompaniment** to the melody.

Legato

The next song contains two curved lines called **slurs.** A slur indicates that the notes written above it (or sometimes below) should be played **legato.** Legato means to play the notes smoothly, so that they sound connected to each other. To play notes legato, keep your finger on the key until you have started to play the next key.

▶ 9   Orange Blossom

This song has dotted half notes in both the left hand part and the right hand part. Play the melody legato.

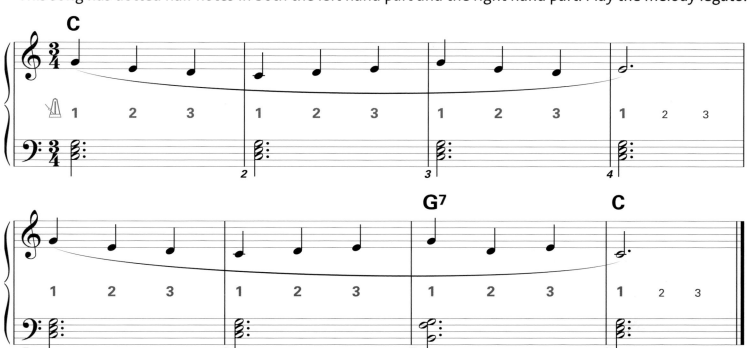

Know Your Keyboards...
Keytar

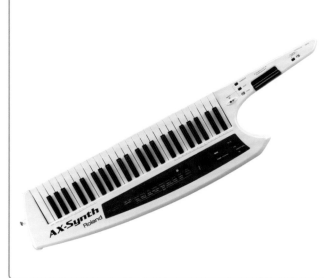

The Keytar is an unusual hybrid instrument, utilizing design elements from both Keyboards and Guitars. It is basically a light-weight Keyboard which can be slung over the shoulder like a guitar while still retaining the playing characteristics of a Keyboard. In most designs, like the Roland AX-7 (pictured), the 'neck' of the Keytar contains controls for pitch bend, sustain and modulation.

The Tie

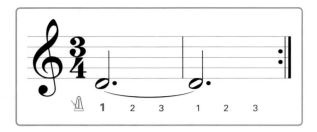

A **tie** is a curved line that connects two notes with the **same** position on the staff. A tie tells you to play the **first** note only, and to hold it for the length of both notes.

 10

Play the **C** note and chord and hold them for **six** beats.

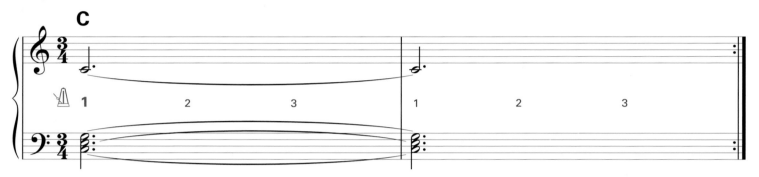

11   Roses From the South

This song was written by **Johann Strauss**, who wrote some of the most famous waltzes. In the melody, a tie is used between bars **15** and **16** (two E notes), and between bars **31** and **32** (two F notes). The tie is also used for the chords in these bars. Do not confuse the tie with the legato slur introduced on the previous page.

Johann Strauss

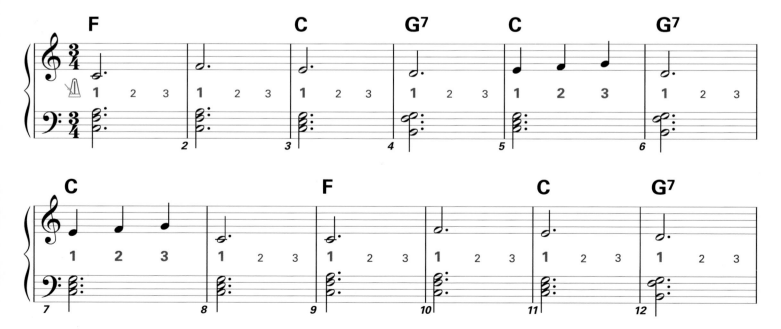

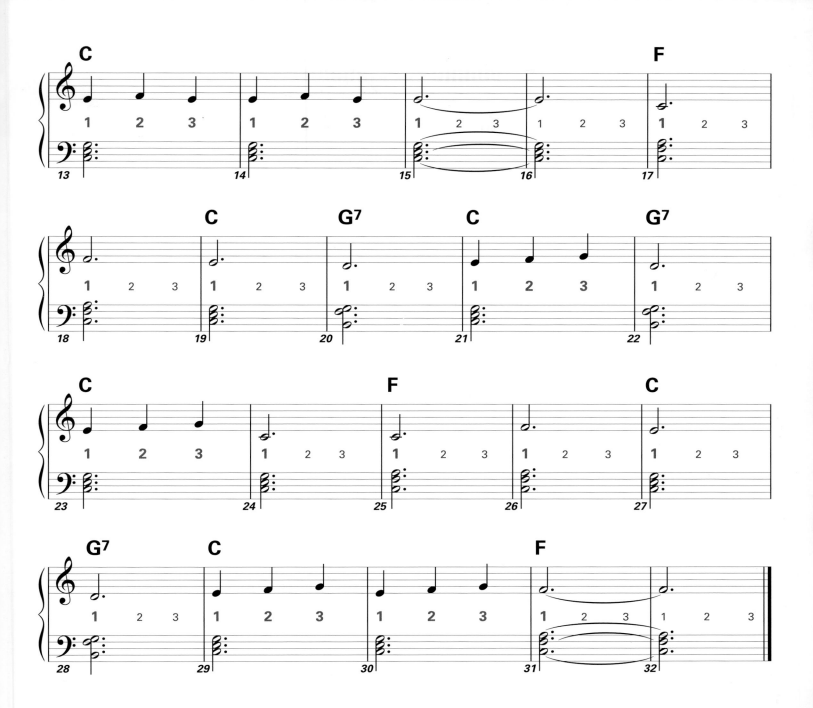

Know Your Keyboards…
Korg OASYS

The Korg OASYS is a high-end software-based workstation synthesizer which contains features more common to a personal computer (PC) than your average Electronic Keyboard, such as a Pentium processor chip, internal hard disk and large LCD touch screen. It uses highly advanced synthesizer technology to provide almost limitless capabilities in the realm of sound production, making this Keyboard very popular for use in the recording studio as well as live performance.

LESSON FIVE

The Notes A, B and C

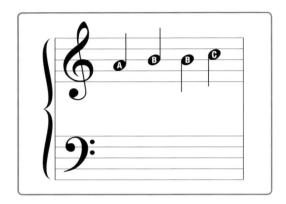

Notes written **above** the middle line of a staff usually have their stems going **down.** Notes written **below** the middle line of the staff usually have their stems going **up.** The stem for the **B** note can go **up or down**.

The C Major Scale

A **major scale** is a group of eight notes that gives the familiar sound:

Do Re Mi Fa So La Ti Do

You now know enough notes to play the **C major scale**. To play the C major scale smoothly you will need to play the **F** note with your **thumb.** Do this by moving your thumb **underneath** your second and third fingers on the way **up** the scale. On the way **down** the scale, move your second and third fingers **over** your thumb. This is called the **crossover.**

The small numbers placed above, below or beside notes on the staves tell you which finger to play each note with. Be sure to use the correct finger.

The Octave

An **octave** is the range of eight notes of a major scale. The **first** note and the **last** note of a major scale always have the **same** name. In the C major scale, the distance from Middle C to the C note above it (or below it) is one octave (eight notes). All the songs you have studied so far, and the next, use notes from the C major scale. Pay close attention to any fingering numbers near the notes. It is important to use the indicated fingering, as this will make the songs easier to play. Use this same fingering every time you play the songs.

13　La Spagnola

La Spagnola uses notes from the **C major scale** and uses the **thumb under** between bars **20** and **21.**

www.learntoplaymusic.com　　　　　　　　　　　PROGRESSIVE BEGINNER KEYBOARD　　23

The Eighth Note

This is an **eighth note**. It lasts for half a **count**. There are eight eighth notes in one bar of $\frac{4}{4}$ time.

Beam

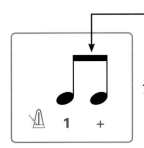

When two or more eighth notes are joined together the tails are replaced by a **beam**.

Two eighth notes joined together.

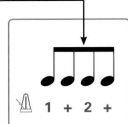

Four eighth notes joined together.

14   How to Count Eighth Notes

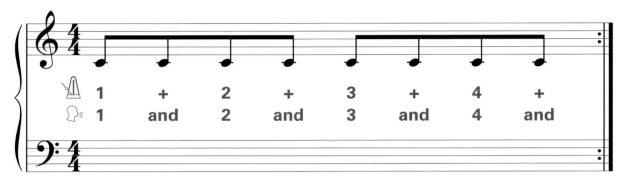

	1	+	2	+	3	+	4	+
	1	and	2	and	3	and	4	and

Staccato

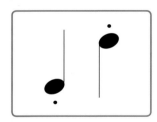

A **dot** placed above or below a note tells you to play it **staccato**. Staccato means to play a note short and separate from other notes. To play a note short, lift your finger off the key as quickly as possible after striking the note.

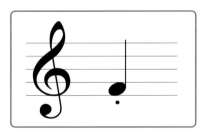

15   Shave and a Haircut

There are two eighth notes on the second beat of the first bar of this example. Play the notes and chords in the second bar staccato.

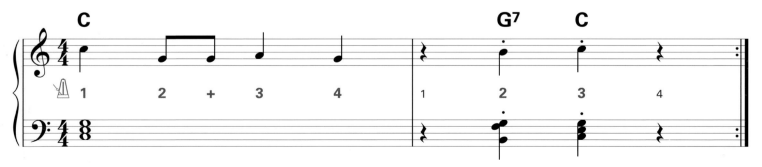

www.learntoplaymusic.com

The Key of C Major

When a song consists of notes from a particular scale, it is said to be written in the **key** which has the **same** name as that scale. For example, if a song contains notes from the **C major scale**, it is said to be in the **key of C major**. Nearly all the songs you have studied so far have been in the key of C major.

 16   **Lavender's Blue**

This well known English folk song is in the key of **C major**. It uses a crossover in bar **14**.

LESSON SIX

The Dotted Quarter Note

A dot written after a quarter note indicates that you should hold the note for **one and a half** beats.

A dotted quarter note is often followed by an eighth note.

17

18   Lullaby

Brahms' Lullaby is one of the most well known melodies of all time. It is written here in the key of **C major** and uses dotted quarter notes in bars **1, 3, 9** and **13**.

Johannes Brahms

www.learntoplaymusic.com

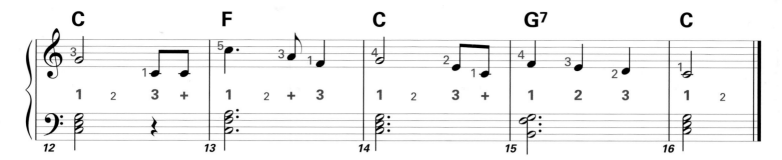

First and Second Endings

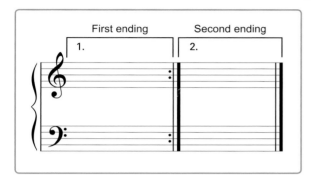

The next song contains **first and second endings**. The **first** time you play through the song, play the **first** ending, (1.), then go back to the beginning. The **second** time you play through the song, play the **second** ending (2.) instead of the first.

 19   **Jingle Bells**

Jingle Bells is one of the most popular Christmas songs. It contains first and second endings. The first time through, play from the beginning to the end of bar **8**. Then play again from the beginning, but this time **do not** play bars 7 and 8 (the first ending), play bars **9** and **10** (the second ending).

Minor Chords

There are three main types of chords: **major**, **seventh** and **minor** chords. You have already learned some major chords and one seventh chord. The first **minor** chord you will learn is the **D minor** chord. Minor chords are indicated by a small "**m**" written after the chord name, e.g., **Dm.**

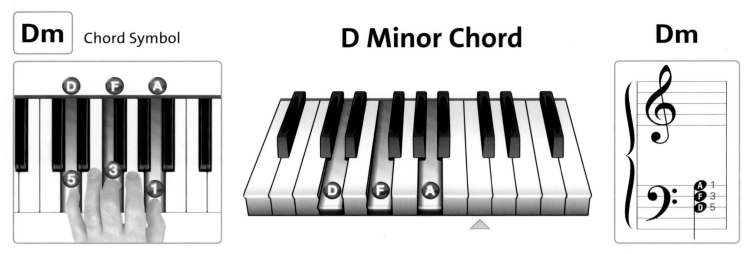

Dm Chord Symbol

D Minor Chord

Dm

The **D minor** chord contains the notes **D**, **F** and **A**. To play the **D minor** chord use the **first**, **third** and **fifth** fingers of your left hand, as shown in the **Dm** chord diagram.

The Common Time Signature

C

This symbol is called **common time**. It means exactly the same as $\frac{4}{4}$.

▶ **20**   **Mussi Den**

This song is in the key of **C major** and contains a **Dm** chord in bar **13**. It also contains two lead-in notes at the beginning of the song.

21   Scarborough Fair

Scarborough Fair is a folk music standard. It contains **D minor** chords and also introduces the **D note** above the C note which is **one octave higher** than middle C. When changing between the **Dm** and **F** chords, keep your **first** finger in position, as it is common to both chords.

LESSON SEVEN

G | Chord Symbol

G Major Chord

G

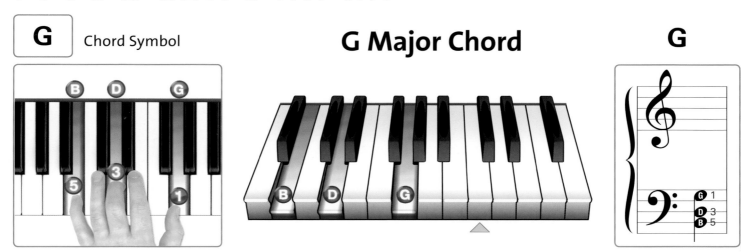

The **G** chord contains the notes **G**, **B** and **D**. To play the **G** chord use the **first**, **third** and **fifth** fingers of your left hand, as shown in the **G** chord diagram.

Sharp Signs

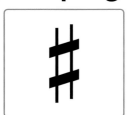

A **sharp** sign raises the note played by **one semitone** (see page 62). On the Keyboard, play the key immediately to the right of the note to play a sharp. When a sharp sign is written on the staff it is always written before the note.

D7 | Chord Symbol

D Seventh Chord

D7

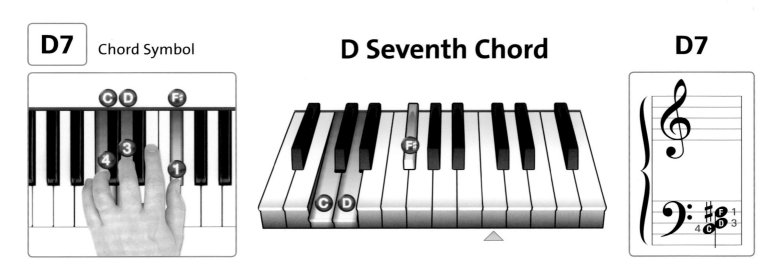

The **D7** chord contains the notes **D**, **F♯** and **C**. To play the **D7** chord use the **first**, **third** and **fourth** fingers of your left hand, as shown in the **D7** chord diagram.

When changing between the **G** and **D7** chords, keep your **third** finger in position as this note is common to both chords.

When changing between the **G** and **D7** chords, keep your **third** finger in position as this note is common to both chords.

 22   Hush Little Baby

This popular children's song makes use of the chords **G** and **D7**.

 23   Tom Dooley

When playing the melody of this song, be careful to play the correct timing in bars **9, 11, 13** and **15**. Practice the timing in these bars separately before playing the complete song.

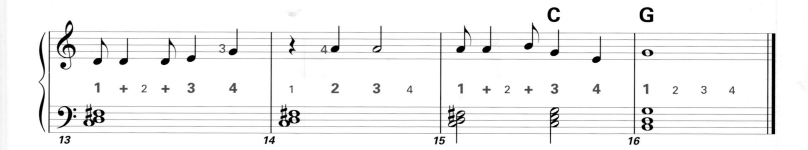

The Eighth Note Triplet

An **eighth note triplet** is a group of three evenly spaced notes played within one beat. Eighth note triplets are indicated by three eighth notes with the number *3* written either above or below the group. Sometimes the triplet has a bracket or a curved line around the number *3*. The notes are played a third of a beat each. Accent (play louder) the first note of each triplet group as it will help you keep time.

▶ 24   Amazing Grace

Amazing Grace is a Gospel song which contains a lead-in and triplets.

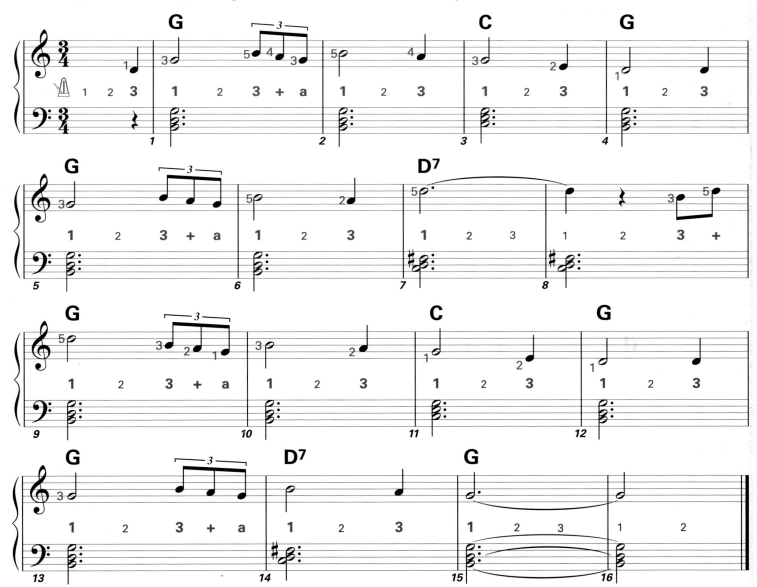

The Note F♯ (above Middle C)

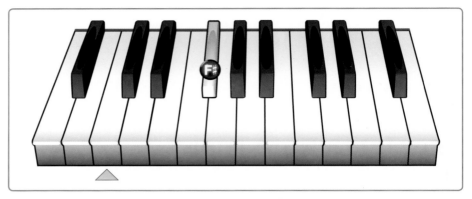

This **F♯** note is written in the **first space** of the treble staff and is the **black** key immediately to the **right** of the F note, as shown in the diagram.

▶ 25   The William Tell Overture

Most of the melody notes in this song are played **staccato** as indicated by the dot placed under or over the note. All the chords are played staccato except for the first **D7** chord in bar 7.

LESSON EIGHT

Turnaround Progressions

A **Turnaround** progression is a set pattern of chords that repeats itself. There are hundreds of well known songs based upon Turnaround progressions. All these songs contain basically the same chords in the same order. A Turnaround may repeat over any number of bars. Usually 2, 4 and 8 bars. However the **chord sequence** remains the same. Some of the biggest hit records of all time are based upon a Turnaround progression. Turnarounds always contain at least one minor chord. The Turnaround below uses a new chord **E minor (Em)**.

 Chord Symbol

E Minor Chord

Em

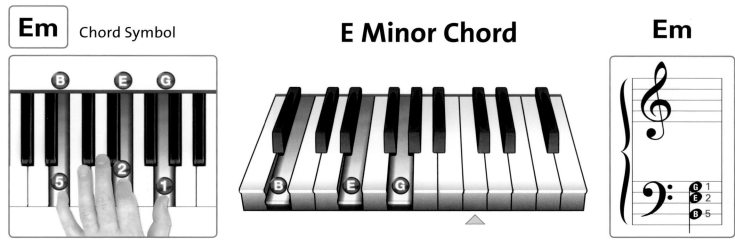

The **E minor** chord contains the notes **E**, **G** and **B**. To play the **E minor** chord use the **first**, **third** and **fifth** fingers of your left hand, as shown in the **Em** chord diagram.

▶ **26**

This progression is a Turnaround in the key of G. It will probably sound familiar to you. To make the left hand part easier to play, use the **first, second** and **fourth** fingers to play the **C** chord in this example.

- When changing between **G** and **Em** chords, keep your **first** and **fifth** fingers in position.
- When changing between **Em** and **C** chords, keep your **first** and **second** fingers in position.
- When changing between **C** and **D7** chords, keep your **fourth** finger in position.

Some songs based on a Turnaround progression are:

Stand by Me - John Lennon
I Will Always Love You - Whitney Houston
Return to Sender - Elvis Presley
All I Have to do is Dream - Everly Brothers
Tell Me Why - The Beatles
Let's Twist Again - Chubby Checker

Be My Baby - The Ronettes
Blue Moon - Various Artists
Everlasting Love - U2
Can't Smile Without You - Barry Manilow
Please Mr Postman - The Beatles

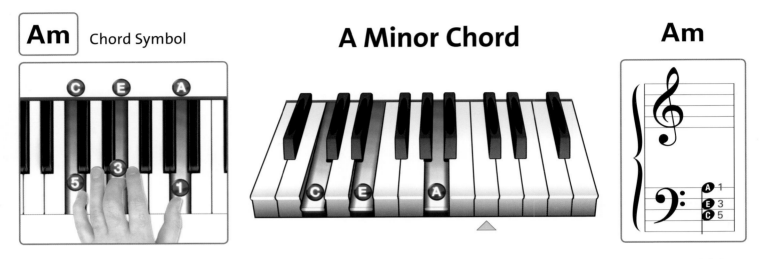

A Minor Chord

Am Chord Symbol

Am

The **A minor** chord contains the notes **A**, **C** and **E**. To play the **A minor** chord use the **first**, **third** and **fifth** fingers of your left hand, as shown in the **Am** chord diagram.

27   Minuet

The melody of this song was a number one hit record and was based on a minuet by famous classical composer **Bach.** It introduces the note **B** below middle C in bars **7** and **15**.

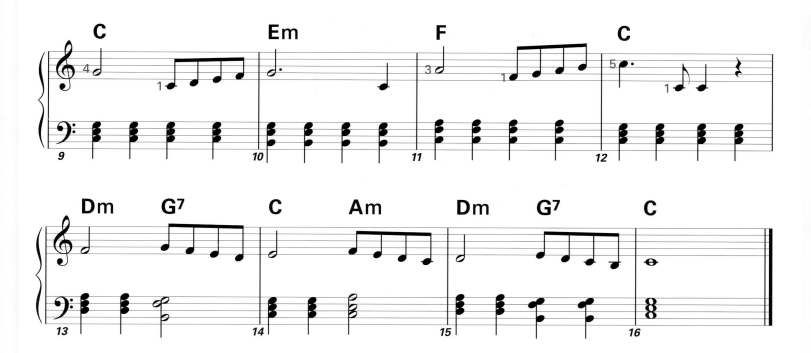

Broken Chords

 28   **Broken Chords**

Sometimes when you play a chord, instead of playing all three notes together, you play the lowest note of the **chord shape** (chord fingering), followed by the other two notes of the chord. The following example demonstrates broken chords in ¾ time using the chords **C**, **F** and **G7**.

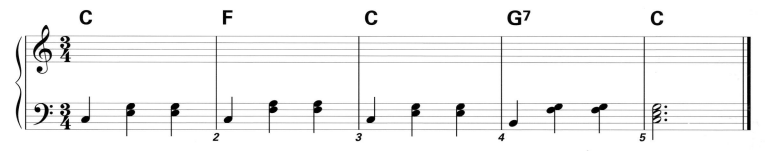

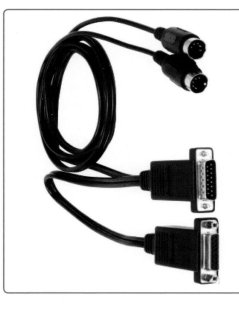

Know Your Keyboards…
MIDI

MIDI (Musical Instrument Digital Interface) is a method of allowing communication between electronic musical instruments, such as Keyboard synthesizers and computers. The way that MIDI differs from connecting a 'line out' from an instrument such as a guitar to an amplifier, or a microphone to a PA, is that no audio signal is transmitted. Instead, a series of computer data is sent through a MIDI cable to compatible hardware or software, where it is then converted into sound.

Here is a new version of the song you learned on page 25, this time using broken chords in the left hand part. Practice the left hand separately at first if necessary.

 30   Morning Has Broken

Morning Has Broken uses all the chords you have learned so far and once again uses broken chords in the left hand part. It also introduces the note **A** below middle C in bar **17**. If you have trouble co-ordinating both hands, practice each hand separately until you are confident playing each part and then combine them.

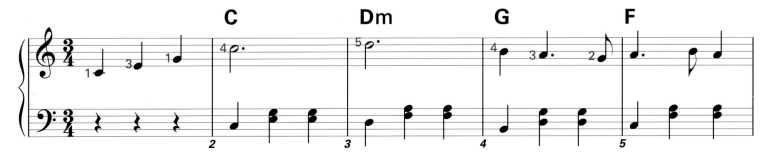

Broken Chords in $\frac{4}{4}$ Time

Broken chords work equally well in $\frac{3}{4}$ time and $\frac{4}{4}$ time. Here are some examples of broken chords in the key of C in $\frac{4}{4}$ time. Once you are comfortable playing them, try applying broken chord accompaniments to some of the other songs you have learned.

This traditional folk song is played with a broken chord accompaniment. Take care with the chord change from **C** to **G7** on the third beat of bars **7** and **15**.

Know Your Keyboards…
Minimoog

The Minimoog is an iconic analog synthesizer produced by the Moog company which became popular with electronic musicians in the early 70's and 80's. The classic sound of the Minimoog (which is able to produce a variety of sounds from a rich bass line to a soaring lead solo) can be heard on many famous recordings by artists such as Pink Floyd and Emerson, Lake & Palmer.

LESSON NINE

The G Major Scale

In Lesson 5 the C Major scale was introduced. The **G major scale** starts and ends on the note **G**, and contains an **F♯** note instead of an F note. Play the following G major scale and notice that it still has the familiar sound **Do Re Mi Fa So La Ti Do**.

The key of C major was discussed on page 25. Songs that use notes from the **C major scale** are said to be in the **key of C major**. Similarly songs that use notes from the **G major scale** are said to be in the **key of G major**. Songs in the key of G will contain **F♯** notes.

Key Signatures

Instead of writing a sharp sign before every F note on the staff, it is easier to write just **one** sharp sign after each clef. This means that **all** the F notes on the staff are played as **F♯**, even though there is no sharp sign written before them. This is called a **key signature**.

The G Major Key Signature

This is the key signature for the key of **G major**. It contains one **F sharp (F♯)** because the G major scale contains **F♯**.

The C Major Key Signature

This is the key signature for the key of **C Major**. It contains **no** sharps or flats because the C major scale contains **no** sharps or flats.

34   I Yi Yi Yi (Cielito Lindo)

I Yi Yi Yi is in the key of **G major**. Notice the key signature and play all F notes as **F♯**. This is one of the most well known songs from Mexico. The left hand accompaniment contains chords played **staccato** in the first part of the song and **broken chords** in the second half.

Arpeggios

On page 37 you were introduced to broken chords. Another useful way of playing chords is **arpeggio style**. An **arpeggio** is a chord played one note at a time. This technique can be applied to **any chord** and can make the accompaniment to a melody much more interesting. The following example demonstrates the chords **C** and **G7** played as arpeggios in ¾ time.

Once you are comfortable playing these chords as arpeggios, try adding a melody with the right hand, as shown in example 36. This is a new arrangement of the song you learned on page 18.

36   Austrian Waltz

Chopsticks is one of the most well known pieces of music for Keyboard. If your hand is not big enough to stretch the octave in bar **7** you can play the whole right hand part of the song using two hands. The left hand part consists of arpeggios of the chords **C** and **G7**. Practice each hand separately at first if you have trouble co-ordinating the two parts. This song is in the key of **C major** as indicated by the key signature (i.e., no sharps or flats).

Arpeggios in $\frac{4}{4}$ Time

Like broken chords, arpeggios work equally well in any time signature. The following examples demonstrate some of the ways arpeggios can be used in $\frac{4}{4}$ time. These examples are written in the key of **G major** as indicated by the key signature.

39   Banks of the Ohio

This time the arpeggios are played as **eighth notes**. The pattern of four notes per chord is exactly the same but they are played over two beats instead of four beats. This may seem difficult at first, but remember that these arpeggios are the **same** chord shapes you already know, played one note at a time. Once again, practice each hand separately at first if necessary.

Sloop John B

This song is in the key of **G major**. There is a **tie** between an eighth note and a quarter note in bar **13**. This gives an "off beat" feel called **syncopation**.

▶ 41 The Sloop John B

www.learntoplaymusic.com

LESSON TEN

Flat Signs

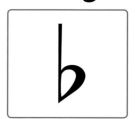

A **flat** sign lowers the note played by **one semitone**.

On the Keyboard, play the key immediately to the left of the note to play a flat. When a flat sign is written on the staff it is always written before the note.

The Note B♭

Two **B flat** notes (written as **B♭**) are shown on the staff below.

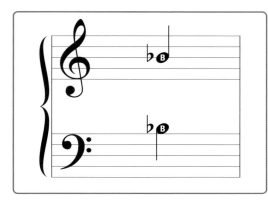

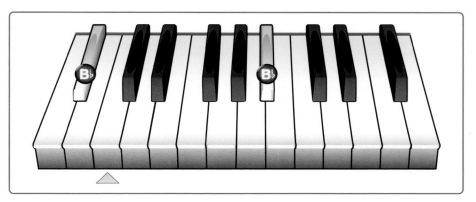

These **B♭** notes are written on the **third** line of the **treble staff** and **second** line of the **bass staff**. The **B♭** note is the **black** key immediately to the **left** of the B note, as shown in the diagram.

12 Bar Blues

12 Bar Blues is a pattern of chords which repeats every 12 bars. There are hundreds of well known songs based on this chord progression, i.e., they contain basically the same chords in the same order.
12 Bar Blues is commonly used in Rock music and is the basis of Blues music.
Some well known Rock and Roll songs which use this 12 bar chord pattern are:

Original Batman T.V. Theme
Hound Dog - Elvis Presley
Rock Around The Clock - Bill Haley
Roll Over Beethoven - Chuck Berry
Blue Suede Shoes - Elvis Presley
In The Mood - Glen Miller

Shake, Rattle and Roll - Bill Haley
Barbara Ann - The Beach Boys
Johnny B. Goode - Chuck Berry
Dizzy Miss Lizzy - The Beatles
Surfin' U.S.A. - The Beach Boys
Good Golly Miss Molly - Little Richard

12 Bar Blues in the Key of C Major

The following 12 Bar Blues is in the key of **C major**, and uses some of the chords you have learned so far. When a song is said to be in the key of C major, it means that the most important chord (and usually the first chord) is the **C** chord.

This pattern of chords will probably sound familiar to you.

42 **12 Bar Blues in the Key of C Major**

The Key of F Major

The **F major scale** starts and ends on the note **F**, and it contains a **B♭** note instead of a B note. Play The F major scale below and listen for the **Do Re Mi Fa So La Ti Do** sound. Songs that use notes from the F major scale are in the **key of F major** and hence contain the note **B♭**.

43

The F Major Key Signature

This is the key signature for the key of **F major**. It contains one **B flat** (B♭) because the F major scale contains B♭.

Instead of writing the flat sign before every B note on the staff, **one** flat sign can be written after each clef. This means that **all** B notes on the staff are played as B♭, even though there is no flat sign written before them.

▶ **44   Marianne**

Marianne is in the key of **F major**. The left hand part here is a variation of the eighth note arpeggio style. Instead of playing the arpeggio straight up and down, the pattern alternates between the lowest note and the other two notes of each chord. This style of accompaniment is very popular in Classical music and is called an **Alberti bass**. Practice the left hand part by itself before combining it with the melody. Listen to the recording to hear how effective the Alberti bass sounds.

The song **Molly Malone** (also called 'Cockles And Mussels') is a well known traditional Irish song and is written below in the key of **F major**. The left hand part is a variation of the Alberti bass pattern, altered to fit in with $\frac{3}{4}$ time. Once again, practice each hand separately at first if necessary. You have now learned all three of the basic methods of accompanying melodies: **chord style**, **broken chord style** and **arpeggio style**. The accompaniment you use can make a big difference to how good the overall piece of music sounds. You can often make a simple melody sound great just by giving it an interesting accompaniment. Go back through the book and experiment with various accompaniments to each of the songs. Remember that each accompaniment style is based on the same basic **chord shapes**.

www.learntoplaymusic.com

APPENDICES

The Keyboard

Major Chord Chart

Minor Chord Chart

Seventh Chord Chart

Minor Seventh Chord Chart

Augmented Chord Chart

Diminished Chord Chart

Glossary of Musical Terms

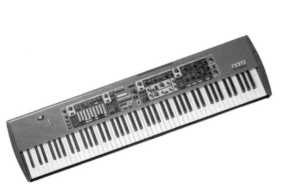

Know Your Keyboards...
Nord ns88

Stage pianos, like the Nord ns88, are Electronic Keyboards designed primarily for live performance. They often feature characteristics of both digital pianos and synthesizers, with weighted-action keys to feel like a real piano, and strong cases to withstand the rigors of touring. They generally contain a small selection of digitally-sampled piano and electric piano sounds, however they are of a higher quality in comparison with Electronic Keyboards designed for home use.

Notes on the Keyboard

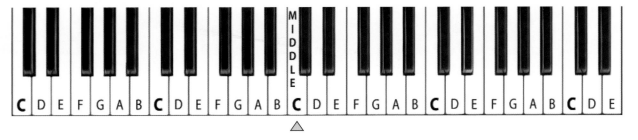

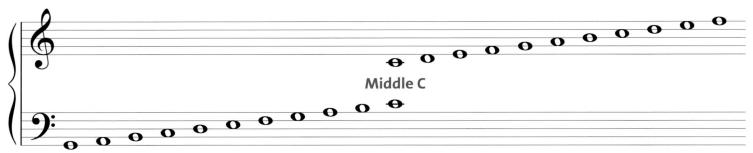

Middle C

Chord Chart

In this book you are introduced to **Major**, **Minor** and **Seventh** chords. The following chord charts contain many other chords you may find in sheet music. Other important chord types are the **Minor Seventh** chord (**m7**), **Augmented** (**+**) and **Diminished** (**o**) chords. These are listed on pages 56, 57 and 58. There are many other types of chords e.g., **Sixth** (**6**), **Suspended** (**sus**), **Ninth** (**9**) etc. The following charts show three different positions for each chord.

A: The **root position** - This shape has the **root note** (i.e., the note the chord is named after) as the **lowest** note of the chord.

B: The **first and second inversions** contain the **same** notes as the root position but have them in a **different** order.

Easy Chord Table

When playing from sheet music and coming across an unfamiliar chord, consult **Progressive Keyboard Chords**, or study the table below to find an easier chord to play. This chord will still sound correct. E.g., when you see a **Cmaj7** symbol, play a **C** chord instead. For a **Cm6**, you can substitute a **Cm** chord, etc.

Chord Written on Sheet Music			Use This Chord
7	-	Seventh	**Major**
6	-	Sixth	
maj7	-	Major Seventh	
sus	-	Suspended	
9	-	9th	**Seventh (7)**
11	-	Eleventh	
13	-	Thirteenth	
m6	-	Minor Sixth	**Minor (m)**
m7	-	Minor Seventh	
m(maj)7 -		Minor Major Seventh	

Major Chord Chart

Chord Name	Notes In Chord	Root Position	First Inversion	Second Inversion
C	C E G			
D♭	D♭ F A♭			
D	D F♯ A			
E♭	E♭ G B♭			
E	E G♯ B			
F	F A C			
F♯	F♯ A♯ C♯			
G	G B D			
A♭	A♭ C E♭			
A	A C♯ E			
B♭	B♭ D F			
B	B D♯ F♯			

Minor Chord Chart

Chord Name	Notes In Chord	Root Position	First Inversion	Second Inversion
Cm	C Eb G			
C#m	C# E G#			
Dm	D F A			
Ebm	Eb Gb Bb			
Em	E G B			
Fm	F Ab C			
F#m	F# A C#			
Gm	G Bb D			
G#m	G# B D#			
Am	A C E			
Bbm	Bb Db F			
Bm	B D F#			

Seventh Chord Chart

Chord Name	Notes In Chord	Root Position	First Inversion (5th omitted)	Second Inversion
C7	C E G Bb			
Db7	Db F Ab Cb			
D7	D F# A C			
Eb7	Eb G Bb Db			
E7	E G# B D			
F7	F A C Eb			
F#7	F# A# C# E			
G 7	G B D F			
Ab7	Ab C Eb Gb			
A 7	A C# E G			
Bb7	Bb D F Ab			
B7	B D# F# A			

Minor Seventh Chord Chart

Chord Name	Notes In Chord	Root Position	First Inversion (5th omitted)	Second Inversion
Cm7	C E♭ G B♭			
C#m7	C# E G# B			
Dm7	D F A C			
E♭m7	E♭ G♭ B♭ D♭			
Em7	E G B D			
Fm7	F A♭ C E♭			
F#m7	F# A C# E			
Gm7	G B♭ D F			
G#m7	G# B D# F#			
Am7	A C E G			
B♭m7	B♭ D♭ F A♭			
Bm7	B D F# A			

Augmented Chord Chart

Chord Name	Notes In Chord		Chord Name	Notes In Chord	
C aug	C E G♯		F♯ aug	F♯ A♯ D	
C♯ aug	C♯ F A		G aug	G B D♯	
D aug	D F♯ A♯		G♯ aug	G♯ C E	
E♭ aug	E♭ G B		A aug	A C♯ F	
E aug	E G♯ C		B♭ aug	B♭ D F♯	
F aug	F A C♯		B aug	B D♯ G	

Know Your Keyboards…

Synthesizers

Synthesizers are electronic instruments which can produce a wide range of sounds through analog or digital means. Early analog synths, like the Roland Jupiter-8, operated by generating audio signals of different frequencies, however most modern synths, like the Roland Fantom-X (pictured) use digital technology to produce sounds. Synthesizers generally incorporate a traditional piano-style Keyboard in their design with additional controls such as buttons and knobs to allow users to modify the sound.

Diminished Chord Chart

Chord Name	Notes In Chord		Chord Name	Notes In Chord

C dim - C E♭ G♭

F♯ dim - F♯ A C

C♯ dim - C♯ E G

G dim - G B♭ D♭

D dim - D F A♭

G♯ dim - G♯ B D

E♭ dim - E♭ G♭ A

A dim - A C E♭

E dim - E G B♭

B♭ dim - B♭ D♭ E

F dim - F A♭ B

B dim - B D F

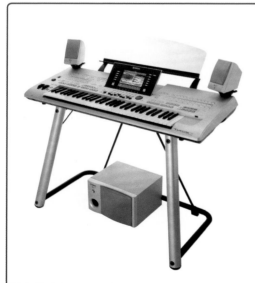

Know Your Keyboards…
Yamaha Tyros

Keyboard workstations like the Yamaha Tyros include a vast array of high-quality sampled instrument sounds and accompaniment styles, making them great for performing solo as a one-man band or providing karaoke backing music. They also often feature easy-to-use recording capabilities, allowing a player to record and produce their own songs and some even include lesson modules which can assist in learning to play the Keyboard.

www.learntoplaymusic.com

Glossary of Musical Terms

Accidental — a sign used to show a temporary change in pitch of a note (i.e., sharp♯, flat♭, double sharp ✕, double flat ♭♭, or natural ♮). The sharps or flats in a key signature are not regarded as accidentals.

Ad lib — to be played at the performer's own discretion.

Allegretto — moderately fast.

Allegro — fast and lively.

Anacrusis — a note or notes occurring before the first bar of music (also called 'lead-in' notes).

Andante — an easy walking pace.

Arpeggio — the playing of a chord in single note fashion.

Bar — a division of music occurring between two barlines (also called a 'measure').

Barline — a vertical line drawn across the staff which divides the music into equal sections called bars.

Bass — the lower regions of pitch in general. On Keyboard, the notes to the left of the Keyboard.

Chord — a combination of three or more different notes played together.

Chord progression — a series of chords played as a musical unit (e.g., as in a song).

Chromatic scale — a scale ascending and descending in semitones.

e.g., **C** chromatic scale:

ascending:	C	C♯	D	D♯	E	F	F♯	G	G♯	A	A♯	B	C
descending:	C	B	B♭	A	A♭	G	G♭	F	E	E♭	D	D♭	C

Clef — a sign placed at the beginning of each staff of music which fixes the location of a particular note on the staff, and hence the location of all other notes, e.g.:

Coda — an ending section of music, signified by the sign ⊕

Common time — an indication of ₄/₄ time — four quarter note beats per bar (also indicated by **C**)

D.C. al fine — a repeat from the sign (indicated thus 𝄋) to the word 'fine'.

Duration — the time value of each note.

Dynamics — the varying degrees of softness (indicated by the term 'piano') and loudness (indicated by the term 'forte') in music.

Eighth note — a note with the value of half a beat in $\frac{4}{4}$ time, indicated thus ♪ (also called a quaver).

The eighth note rest — indicating half a beat of silence is written: ⁊

Enharmonic — describes the difference in notation, but not in pitch, of two notes: e.g.:

F♯ or G♭

Fermata — a sign, ⌢ , used to indicate that a note or chord is held to the player's own discretion (also called a 'pause sign').

First and second endings — signs used where two different endings occur. On the first time through, ending one is played (indicated by the bracket ⌐1.⌐); then the progression is repeated and ending two is played (indicated by ⌐2.⌐).

Flat — a symbol, (♭) used to lower the pitch of a note by one semitone.

Forte — loud. Indicated by the sign $\boldsymbol{f}$

Half note — a note with the value of two beats in $\frac{4}{4}$ time, indicated thus: ♩ (also called a minim). The half note rest, indicating two beats of silence, is written: ▬ on the third staff line.

Harmony — the simultaneous sounding of two or more different notes.

Improvise — to perform spontaneously; i.e., not from memory or from a written copy.

Interval — the distance between any two notes of different pitches.

Key — describes the notes used in a composition in regards to the major or minor scale from which they are taken; e.g., a piece 'in the key of C major' describes the melody, chords, etc., as predominantly consisting of the notes, **C, D, E, F, G, A,** and **B** — i.e., from the **C** scale.

Key signature — a sign, placed at the beginning of each stave of music, directly after the clef, to indicate the key of a piece. The sign consists of a certain number of sharps or flats, which represent the sharps or flats found in the scale of the piece's key, e.g.:

 This indicates a scale with **F♯** and **C♯**, which is **D** major; **D E F♯ G A B C♯ D.** Therefore the key is **D** major (or its relative minor, **Bm**).

Lead-In — same as anacrusis (also called a pick-up).

Ledger lines — small horizontal lines upon which notes are written when their pitch is either above or below the range of the staff, e.g.:

Legato — smoothly, well connected.

Lyrics — words that accompany a melody.

Major scale — a series of eight notes in alphabetical order based on the interval sequence tone - tone - semitone - tone - tone - tone - semitone, giving the familiar sound **Do Re Mi Fa So La Ti Do**.

Melody — a succession of notes of varying pitch and duration which has a recognizable musical shape.

Metronome — a device which indicates the number of beats per minute, and which can be adjusted in accordance to the desired tempo.

e.g., **MM** (Maelzel Metronome) ♩= 60 — indicates 60 quarter note beats per minute.

Moderato — at a moderate pace.

Natural — a sign (♮)used to cancel out the effect of a sharp or flat. The word is also used to describe the notes **A, B, C, D, E, F** and **G**; e.g., 'the natural notes'.

Notation — the written representation of music, by means of symbols (music on a staff), letters (as in chord and note names) and diagrams (as in chord illustrations.)

Note — a single sound with a given pitch and duration.

Octave — the distance between any given note with a set frequency, and another note with exactly double that frequency. Both notes will have the same letter name;

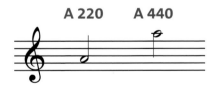

Pitch — the sound produced by a note, determined by the frequency of the string vibrations. The pitch relates to a note being referred to as 'high' or 'low'.

Quarter note — a note with the value of one beat in $\frac{4}{4}$ time, indicated thus ♩ (also called a crotchet). The quarter note rest, indicating one beat of silence, is written: 𝄽

Repeat signs — in music, used to indicate a repeat of a section of music, by means of two dots placed before a double bar line:

In chord progressions, a repeat sign ✕ , indicates an exact repeat of the previous bar.

Rhythm — the natural pattern of strong and weak pulses in a piece of music.

Riff — a pattern of notes that is repeated throughout a progression (song).

Root note — the note after which a chord or scale is named.

Scale Tone Chords — chords which are constructed from notes within a given scale.

Semitone — the smallest interval used in conventional music. On the Keyboard, each key represents one semitone.

Sharp — a sign (♯) used to raise the pitch of a note by one semitone.

Simple time — occurs when the beat falls on an undotted note, which is thus divisible by two.

Sixteenth note — a note with the value of a quarter of a beat in $\frac{4}{4}$ time, indicated as such ♪ (also called a semiquaver).

Sixteenth note rest — indicates a quarter of a beat of silence, is written: 𝄿

Slur — a curved line which indicates that the notes written above (or sometimes below) it, should be played legato.

Staccato — to play short and detached. Indicated by a dot placed above the note:

Staff — five parallel lines together with four spaces, upon which music is written.

Syncopation — the placing of an accent on a normally unaccented beat. e.g.:

Tempo — the speed of a piece.

Tie — a curved line joining two or more notes of the same pitch, where the second note(s) is not played, but its time value is added to that of the first note.

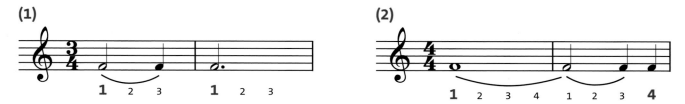

Timbre — a quality which distinguishes a note produced on one instrument from the same note produced on any other instrument (also called 'tone color'). A given note on the Keyboard will sound different (and therefore distinguishable) from the same pitched note on piano, violin, flute etc. There is usually also a difference in timbre from one Keyboard to another.

Time signature — a sign at the beginning of a piece which indicates, by means of figures, the number of beats per bar (top figure), and the type of note receiving one beat (bottom figure).

Tone — a distance of two keys; i.e., the equivalent of two semitones.

Transposition — the process of changing music from one key to another.

Treble — the upper regions of pitch in general.

Treble clef — a sign placed at the beginning of the staff to fix the pitch of the notes placed on it. The treble clef (also called 'G clef') is placed so that the second line indicates a G note:

Tremolo — A technique involving rapid repetition of a given note or notes.

Triplet — a group of three notes played in the same time as two notes of the same kind.

Vibrato — A feature on some Electronic Keyboards which rapidly fluctuates the pitch of a note.

Whole note — a note with the value of four beats in $\frac{4}{4}$ time, indicated thus $\mathbf{o}$ (also called a semibreve).

Progressive Beginner Blues Harmonica

FOR BEGINNING BLUES HARMONICA PLAYERS

An informative, easy to follow introduction to the world of Blues Harmonica. Introduces cross harp playing immediately and covers essential techniques such as note bending, vibrato, slides, train rhythms, call and response and improvisation.

Progressive Beginner Electronic Keyboard

FOR BEGINNER KEYBOARD PLAYERS

An easy to follow Electronic Keyboard method for the complete beginner. Covers note reading, finger technique, using the automatic accompaniment function and playing chords with the left hand. Includes many well known songs in a variety of styles.

Progressive Beginner Recorder

FOR BEGINNING RECORDER PLAYERS

A great introduction to the fundamentals of Recorder playing and understanding music. All examples sound great and are fun to play. Covers a variety of styles including Classical, Jazz, Blues, Pop and Rock in four major keys and three minor keys.

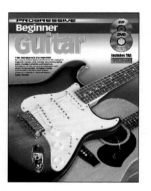

Progressive Beginner Guitar

FOR BEGINNER GUITAR STUDENTS

An easy to follow Guitar method for the complete beginner. Covers both melody and chord playing using standard notation and tablature. Introduces all the essential techniques and music fundamentals. Includes chords and melodies of many well known songs in a variety of musical styles.

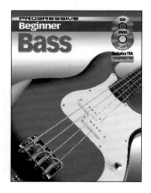

Progressive Beginner Bass

FOR BEGINNER BASS PLAYERS

An easy and informative introduction to playing the Electric Bass. The emphasis is on making music right from the start. Includes all the essential techniques and music fundamentals as they apply to bass playing.